Community Questions

HOW CAN PEOPLE HELP COMMUNITIES?

by Martha E. H. Rustad

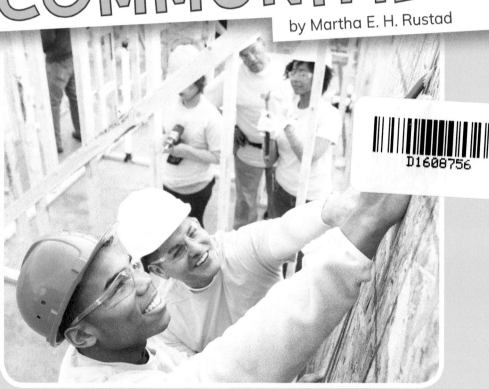

D1608756

PEBBLE
a capstone imprint

Pebble Emerge is published by Pebble, an imprint of Capstone.
1710 Roe Crest Drive, North Mankato, Minnesota 56003
www.capstonepub.com

Library of Congress Cataloging-in-Publication Data is available on the Library of Congress website.
ISBN 978-1-9771-2270-4 (library binding)
ISBN 978-1-9771-2610-8 (paperback)
ISBN 978-1-9771-2297-1 (eBook PDF)
Summary: A community is only as strong as its individual members. What roles do those members play, and how do citizens work together to complete common tasks and achieve goals? A clear question-and-answer format, paired with photos kids can relate to, shows the importance of responsibility and cooperation. A simple activity encourages young readers to actively participate in their own community.

Image Credits
Getty Images: BSIP, 11; iStockphoto: kali9, 5, monkeybusinessimages, 14, SDI Productions, 1; Shutterstock: Becky Starsmore, top 20, CREATISTA, 17, donatas1205, bottom 20, ESB Professional, 7, justaa, (icon) cover, joseph s l tan matt, 16, Leonard Zhukovsky, 9, Monkey Business Images, 10, 12, 15, New Africa, 13, Pixel-Shot, Cover, Rafal Olechowski, 6, Rawpixel.com, 19, Victoria Kalinina, design element

Editorial Credits
Editor: Jill Kalz; Designer: Juliette Peters; Media Researcher: Morgan Walters; Production Specialist: Kathy McColley

All internet sites appearing in back matter were available and accurate when this book was sent to press.

Table of Contents

Who Helps a Community? 4

How Can We Help Our
Community Spaces? 6

How Can We Help Others
in Our Community? 10

How Can We Make Our
Community Stronger? 16

Get Involved:
Message Rocks 20

Glossary 22

Read More 23

Internet Sites 23

Index 24

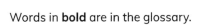

Words in **bold** are in the glossary.

Who Helps a Community?

A **community** is a group of people.

They live, work, and play together.

Everyone wants to live in a safe place.

We want to be happy and healthy too.

To get those things, we work together.

Each of us can help our community.

How Can We Help Our Community Spaces?

Community spaces are places we share. **Neighborhoods** and parks are shared. So are sidewalks and roads. We want our shared spaces to be clean and safe.

Together we pick up trash. We keep
sidewalks clear of snow and ice. We fill
holes in the roads. We fix things that
are broken. We keep our spaces well lit.

We want our community to look nice. Some people plant pretty flower gardens. Others plant colorful vegetables to share. Artists may paint **murals** on buildings. The paintings often tell a story about the community and why it is special.

How Can We Help Others in Our Community?

We make our community better by helping other people. We may cook food for people to eat at a community center. We may bring food to people's homes.

Some teachers take kids to **nursing homes**. The kids spend time with the people who live there. They make art. They sing, dance, tell stories, and laugh.

Some people help at the library. They put books on shelves. They help other people find what they need. They read to kids. Everyone feels welcome.

We help animals in our community too. **Volunteers** play with dogs and cats at the shelter. They clean cages. They give love and care to the animals.

Sometimes new people move to our community. We are friendly. We talk to them. We show them around our town or city. We help them meet other people.

We can all help others by being kind.
Let everyone share their ideas. Listen
when others speak. Use good manners.
Make others feel like they belong.

How Can We Make Our Community Stronger?

Working together makes us stronger. Playing together does too! Community **festivals** are fun. Everyone enjoys helping in some way.

Community leaders start with a plan. Workers set up tables and chairs. They cook lots of food. People listen to music. They sing, dance, and make new friends.

We help our community in many ways. Everyone can do something. We keep our shared spaces clean and safe. We work together. We share ideas, and we listen. We care for others. How can you help your community?

Get Involved: Message Rocks

It's important to be kind. Share this message with your community by painting rocks.

What You Need:
- clean, flat rocks
- waterproof paint
- paintbrushes
- toothpicks

What You Do:

1. Paint one side of a rock a light color.
2. Once the paint dries, use a paintbrush or toothpick to write a kind message on the rock. Start with one of these: Be Kind, Smile, Make a New Friend, Dream.
3. Repeat steps 1 and 2 until all the rocks are painted.
4. Ask an adult to help you place the rocks around your community. Try parks, playgrounds, or along walking trails. Then watch the kindness spread!

Glossary

community (kuh-MYOO-nuh-tee)—a group of people who live, work, and play together

festival (FESS-tuh-vuhl)—a well-planned party, often held every year at the same time

mural (MYUR-uhl)—a painting on a wall

neighborhood (NAY-bur-hood)—a small area in a town or city where people live

nursing home (NUR-sing hohm)—a place that gives care to people who can't care for themselves

volunteer (vol-uhn-TEER)—a person who helps without getting paid

Read More

Emminizer, Theresa. *You're Part of a Neighborhood Community!* New York: Gareth Stevens, 2020.

Reeves, Diane Lindsey. *Making Choices in My Community.* Ann Arbor, MI: Cherry Lake Publishing, 2018.

Internet Sites

Be a Volunteer
https://kidshealth.org/en/kids/volunteering.html?WT.ac=p-ra

Kids Ecology Corps
https://www.kidsecologycorps.org/how-you-can-help

Index

animal shelters, 13

cleaning, 7, 13, 18

festivals, 16–17

food sharing, 10, 17

gardens, 8

libraries, 12

manners, 15

neighborhoods, 6

new people, 14, 17

nursing homes, 11

paintings, 8

parks, 6

playing together, 4, 16, 17

roads, 6, 7

sidewalks, 6, 7

working together, 4, 7, 16, 17, 18